Ambrose Weston

Two Letters Describing a Method of Increasing the Quantity of Circulating-money, upon a new and solid principle

Ambrose Weston

Two Letters Describing a Method of Increasing the Quantity of Circulating-money, upon a new and solid principle

ISBN/EAN: 9783744728812

Printed in Europe, USA, Canada, Australia, Japan

Cover: Foto ©Suzi / pixelio.de

More available books at **www.hansebooks.com**

TWO LETTERS,

DESCRIBING

A METHOD

OF

Increasing the Quantity

OF

CIRCULATING-MONEY:

Upon a new and solid Principle.

———◆———

LONDON: 1799.

Printed by *A. Strahan, Printers Street, Gough Square*

A METHOD

OF

Increasing the Quantity

OF

CIRCULATING-MONEY:

Upon a new and solid Principle.

LETTER I.

CONTENTS.

A 2

INTRODUCTION.

THE PRINCIPLE of this Propofal is to put a NEW and GREAT CAPITAL into CIRCU-LATION, by LOANS of MONEY, to be *created* in the manner and upon the foundation defcribed in the following LETTER, addreffed to a Member of the late SECRET COMMITTEE of the HOUSE of COMMONS on BANK AFFAIRS.

THE gentleman, to whom the Letter was ad-dreffed, (whofe name, if I thought myfelf at liberty to mention it, would add much authority to the whole propofal,) being himfelf ftruck with the no-velty of the meafure, and its apparent tendency to public utility, has been the means of procuring a confiderable degree of favour to it ELSEWHERE. —But, if I were to fay more of this, it could only be with a view to obtain attention,—not to in-fluence the *public judgment*, which alone can de-cide in this cafe, as in all others where PUBLIC CREDIT is concerned.—Therefore, I fhall only fay, I have good reafon to think that the *firft impreffions, impreſſions,* made in the quarter to which I allude, are ſtill RETAINED.

IT is my intention to point out in a future Letter, for which I have prepared materials, how I propoſe to confine the increaſe of money, in its firſt application, to the aſſiſtance of the LANDED INTEREST; and I ſhall, at the ſame time, anſwer ſuch OBJECTIONS as I may hear of, or which my own thoughts may ſuggeſt to me; for, I ſhall diſguiſe nothing.—In the mean time, I admit that it is neceſſary to the PRACTICAL EXECUTION of the plan, that the notes in queſtion ſhould be EXCHANGEABLE for ALL commodities,—by no means excepting GOLD; *and exchangeable* AT PAR : otherwiſe they cannot perform the office of MONEY.— I beg permiſſion to add, that I think this may be ACCOMPLISHED. And I ſhall ſhew how the SECURITY may be DOUBLED, both in its *nature* and *amount,* without leſſening the ſimplicity of the original deſign; and this to the extent of proving it to be ABSOLUTELY IMPOSSIBLE that the Note-Creditors ſhould be *defrauded,* or *even diſappointed,* SO LONG as any notion of LAW and PROPERTY ſhall continue practically to prevail in GREAT BRITAIN.

LONDON,
23d April 1799.

A
M E T H O D,

&c. &c. &c.

Sect. I.—*Assumes the Necessity of an Extension of the Circulating Medium.*

SIR,

Of late, we have heard but little of the plans for a New Circulating Medium, with which the public attention was much engaged about the time of the Bank's ceasing to make payments in cash. No plan of that kind seems yet to have obtained general approbation; and, perhaps, that which I am about to submit to your confideration may not be free from objection.

I have entered thus upon the subject without ceremony; becaufe, Sir, the indulgence you have fhewn me in the feveral conferences you have honoured me with on the occafion, has fuperfeded the neceffity of any introductory matter, unlefs I
had

had attempted to exprefs the feeling I have of your obliging attention in this inftance, which I decline, as a tafk not eafy in itfelf, and ftill lefs fo, in connection with other acts of condefcenfion which I cannot fail to recollect, though I am not able to acknowledge them in the manner I fhould wifh to do.

In common with all thofe who have preceded me in this track, I begin with affuming that there would be found great convenience in the eftablifhment of a good, folid, circulating medium, upon a more enlarged fcale than any that exifts at prefent, and adapted to the extended and extending ftate of our NATIONAL COMMERCE, and particularly to the wants of the LANDED INTEREST. If this was denied, or generally doubted, I fhould have little to fay at prefent; for, if the neceffity or utility of fuch an eftablifhment is not felf-evident, I fhould think the time for it is not yet come.

My experience in bufinefs, however, informs me that it is wanted.—Permanent loans of money are now, and for a long time have been, difficult to be obtained; and this difficulty muft, from obvious caufes, continue to increafe fo long as the war lafts.

SECT. II.—*Bafis of a Plan for fuch an Extenfion.*

HAVING premifed this, I proceed to ftate my plan for the eftablifhment of a New Circulating Medium.

THE bafis of it, as I have remarked in what you have heard from me already, I fix upon the NA-TIONAL DEBT, which is the WEALTH of INDIVI-DUALS.—For commercial purpofes at leaft, I conceive this may be deemed folid fubftantial property —to a limited extent.

SUPPOSE the National Debt due to individuals to be equal to FOUR HUNDRED MILLIONS (or more) of 3 per Cent. Annuities of the value of 50 per cent.; that is, TWO HUNDRED MILLIONS fterling. This fuppofition is fufficiently accurate for my prefent purpofe.

SECT. III.—*The Plan ftated.*

Now, my fcheme goes to the putting of a large portion, FIFTY MILLIONS, or more, of this property into circulation, if fo much could be em-

B   ployed;

ployed; and this I propofe to be done in the following manner:

LET any ſtock-holder, who would wiſh to circulate ſome part of his STOCK, without ſelling it,
transfer a certain quantity of it, ſuppoſe twenty
thouſand pounds 3 per Cents. to the GOVERNORS
and DIRECTORS of the BANK. The Bank is then
to deliver to him fifty certificates, or notes of the
transfer, each of them to be marked as of the value
of £.100, or a greater quantity in number, and of
leſs value reſpectively; but the whole together to
be of the amount of £.5000 ſterling.

BY this means every particular quantity of ſtock
might produce a fourth part of its nominal amount
for the purpoſes of circulation. For, I make what
I believe to be a well-grounded ſuppoſition, that the
mercantile world, who now take BANK-NOTES in
payment, would, with equal confidence, receive
and circulate theſe STOCK-NOTES; the Governors
and Directors of the Bank of England being, in re-
ſpect to the ſtock to be transferred to them, truſtees
for thoſe who transfer the ſtock, and for thoſe who
take the ſtock-notes in payment, (as they now are
truſtees for the Bank-Proprietors and the holders of
Bank-notes,) and the ſecurity being fully equal to
that

that upon which the credit of Bank-notes is founded:—for, the capital and other effects of the Bank
(reckoning its property in stock at the present
market-rate) is certainly short of twice the amount
of its debts. But the stock, transferred as I propose, would be double in value to the notes circulated upon its credit.

In the case I have suggested, the 3 per Cents.
would be taken at 25; a supposition low enough,
I should suppose, for those who give any degree of
credit whatever to the PUBLIC FUNDS. There can
be no doubt that bankers and others would allow
£.100 stock to be a sufficient security for £.25
money, notwithstanding all the possible fluctuations
to which the stocks are subject.

THE notes I have described might be used for
loans or for capitals to trade upon; their use in
trade, and for other purposes, being supposed the
same as specie or Bank-notes.

THESE notes being, by supposition, of the same
value, and passing with the same facility as Bank-
notes do, will be considered as CASH, and conse-
quently, if lent by the original holders, or by
any others who may become the holders of them,
would entitle the lender to receive INTEREST on

the

the loan, in like manner as the lender of bank-notes now receives interest on the loan of those notes.

THE supposition that these notes would be circulated like bank-notes is essential to my plan.— That foundation taken away, the whole would be an unsubstantial vision ; and therefore, if this be not assented to, it would be of no use for me to go on. But, that point granted, (subject to re-consideration,) I say that every particular quantity of stock, transferred in the manner I have stated, would yield a profit to the stock-transferrer equal to 5 per cent. on the amount of stock-notes obtained by him.

TWENTY THOUSAND POUNDS, 3 per Cent. stock, would, as observed before, produce £. 5000 of stock-notes, the interest of which would be £. 250, to be added to £. 600, the amount of the dividends on £. 20,000 of that stock. Thus £. 850 would be gained annually, instead of £. 600, by every proprietor of £. 20,000 stock, who should avail himself of the opportunity of procuring stock-notes, as above mentioned.

WHAT I have said of 3 per Cent. stock, is to be applied to the *other* public funds in the like proportion ;

proportion; the 3 per Cents. being mentioned only by way of example.

SECT. IV.—*Confequences of the Plan to Stock-Proprietors.*

I SHALL purfue the fuppofition thus made, and fhall trace its confequences to the ftock-proprietor, treating the matter at prefent as if no other intereft than his was to be confulted; difregarding, therefore, at this moment, the interefts of GOVERNMENT and the BANK OF ENGLAND, both of which I fhall feparately confider in what I have farther to fay. In this point of view, I fuppofe the whole dividends on the ftock are to continue payable to the ftock-transferers; a fuppofition to be corrected in the farther progrefs of this difcuffion.

£. 850 being gained annually inftead of £. 600, the value of ftock may be expected to rife in proportion to the increafe of gain.

IN the fubfequent details on this point, I fhall fuppofe the ftock-proprietor would transfer his ftock to the truftees, upon my plan, for the fake of much lefs advantage than what I have above defcribed; for, out of the great profit above alluded to, it is neceffary to provide inducements

to

to Government and to the Bank of England to countenance the plan.

At prefent I fhall proceed to attend farther to the interefts of the ftock-proprietor.

What objection can *he* make? Can he fay his ftock is *tied up* and put out of his power? No: —he may redeem it by bringing in to the Bank a quantity of ftock-notes equal in amount to thofe originally obtained by him. Thefe being cancelled, his ftock would be again entirely free: or he may fell the ftock fubject to the charge upon it: this would make it *light* to hold; which, by rendering the ftock more marketable, would increafe its value.

Merchants, bankers, country-gentlemen, farmers, and in general ftock-holders of all defcriptions, would be benefited by the plan, and particularly the *timid* would derive encouragement to *hold on* their *ftock*. For if they withdraw half the amount of the prefent price of ftock, they may realize that part on land, by procuring purchafes or mortgages. This would alfo accommodate thofe who want to fell land, or borrow money on it, or to borrow on other fecurity.

The

THE transferrer would retain to himſelf the advantage of future increaſe of price, juſt as if he had not taken the ſtock-notes.

SECT. V.—*No Danger to them.*

BUT is there no final danger of loſs to the ſtock-proprietor upon this plan? *None*, I think. For ſuppoſe the holders of the ſtock-notes ſhould become alarmed for their ſecurity by the falling of ſtock to 25; and ſuppoſe the plan ſhould provide, that then the ſtock ſhould, at that price, become the property of the holders of the ſtock-notes, and be transferred to them in proportion to the amount of the notes held by them reſpectively, unleſs redeemed immediately by the proprietors of the ſtock; it may be made clear, that he that was the original ſtock-holder cannot be hurt by having received the notes, even though he ſhould not redeem the ſtock. For if he has retained the right of redemption, and conſequently the riſk, it is by his own voluntary act that he has done ſo. He might have ſold out; but, having retained the ſtock, he cannot ſuffer more by parting with his ſtock now, than if he had held it on, and was now to ſell it, without having received any ſtock-notes. He may even have an advantage by buying an equal

quantity

quantity of the ſtock at the reduced price, ſuppoſing it below 25, or prevent a loſs if the price is 25, or upwards; and, upon both ſuppoſitions, five thouſand pounds, or thereabouts, would replace his twenty thouſand pounds ſtock.

Four things muſt concur in order to occaſion any actual loſs to the transferrer of ſtock upon this plan. Firſt; the ſtock muſt fall below 25. Secondly; the transferrer muſt be unable to redeem it at that reduced rate. Thirdly; the ſtock muſt afterwards riſe to a higher price. Fourthly; if there be (as of courſe there muſt be) an interval of time between the fall and the riſe, the tranferrer muſt continue, during the whole interval, unable to purchaſe a quantity of ſtock equal to what he had when he obtained the notes.

The occurrence and operation of theſe numerous cauſes is a moſt improbable ſuppoſition; eſpecially conſidering that the transferrer muſt be underſtood to have received an equivalent in property of ſome kind on parting with his notes, and, therefore, may be expected to be able to redeem his ſtock, or to buy an equal quantity at the ſuppoſed price of 25.

But perhaps the ſtock-notes may have been applied to purchaſe land or land-tax.—*Well*, at
leaſt

leaſt the transferrer has then realized half the amount of his ſtock at the preſent price, beſides the annual increaſe of £. 250 upon his £. 20,000: and he muſt conſider that, if he had continued to hold his ſtock till the ſuppoſed period of ultimate depreciation, his loſs would be greater than it can be upon any ſuppoſition affecting this plan ; which includes the annual gain of £. 250 upon the £. 20,000 ſtock.

SECT. VI.—*They might gain too much by it.*

IF, according to the ſuppoſition above made, fifty millions could thus be brought into circulation, the gain to the ſtock-holders would be £. 2,500,000 ſterling annually, and ſo in proportion, if the circulating medium ſhould be uſed in leſs or greater extent.

BUT two millions five hundred thouſand pounds would be too great a gain for the ſtock-holder, who could not reaſonably expect to have ſo much, eſpecially if the ſcheme be attended with only part of the other advantages (including that of ſafety) which I have ſtated.

SECT. VII.—*Government must partake with them in the Profits.*

THEREFORE I come now to confider the interests of GOVERNMENT and the BANK OF ENGLAND.

IT may be thought proper that fo much of the dividends as is equal to 5 per cent. on the stock-notes should be kept back by Government: that is, that the payment of fo much of the dividends should be fufpended during the war, and that the amount of thefe dividends should at the end of the war be divided between the stock-holders, the Government, and the Bank of England, in fuch proportions as may be agreed upon. In fpeaking of the stock-holder in this place, I mean the perfon who should actually poffefs the stock at that period; and his share of the accumulated dividends should then be added to his capital, and the future interest of it provided for by taxes, unlefs Government should then be able to pay the arrears of dividends; I mean the stock-holder's share of thofe dividends. In cafe a fufpenfion of dividends should be thought improper, fome other arrangement might be adopted, as the mutual interests of Government and the stock-proprietors might dictate.

IF

IF Government could, by this means, fufpend during the war the payment of dividends to the amount of two millions five hundred thoufand pounds, or even half of that fum, fuch a poftponement, or any equivalent advantage to Government, would be attended with important confequences.

FUTURE LOANS might be negociated on better terms, the price of ftocks being fuppofed to rife as well in confequence of the advantages given to the ftock-transferrers, as of the taking of a great quantity of ftock out of the market. The RE-DEMPTION of the LAND-TAX would be facilitated, and the neceffity to fell ftock would be very much diminifhed, at the fame time that there would be a great increafe of inducements to buy and hold ftock.

SECT. VIII.—*So muft the Bank of England.*

IN regard to the BANK of ENGLAND, the advantages to be allotted to that company would be fuch as might be agreed upon between them and the ftock-transferrers, by way of an annual increafe of the BANK PROFITS; and alfo as a compenfation for the charges of management. But there is no occafion at prefent to enter into details upon this part of the fubject.

AFTER ALL, however, there remains the question before suggested : " Could these STOCK-NOTES be " used as a Circulating Medium; or, in other words, " would they pass as MONEY ?"

THIS I cannot determine ; but I see many considerations which may be supposed to operate towards causing the free and general currency of these notes.

THE security upon which the notes are to circulate, would be a FIRST MORTGAGE on the PROPERTY and INDUSTRY of the NATION. The scheme would raise the value of the funds, and would advance our AGRICULTURE, as well as extend our TRADE, both foreign and domestic, by bringing into action a new and great CAPITAL : and all this would tend to improve the STRENGTH of the NATION. Hence greater SAFETY to every part of our property.

THESE appear to me to be sufficiently powerful inducements to the public to receive and circulate *as Cash* the proposed stock-notes.

BUT

BUT if, in fact, the fecurity for the National Debt is not to be efteemed good for a fourth part of its nominal amount, then, I fear, our cafe is hopelefs indeed. This, however, appears to me to be a groundlefs apprehenfion.

AT all events, the caution of the moft fearful muft have fome limits; and if, through the prevalence of diftruft, the notes defcribed could not be circulated at 25, they might undoubtedly at fome lower rate. Therefore, the objection founded on fuppofed infecurity, does not reach the principle of the meafure, and can only at the utmoft confine its operation.

SECT. X.—*The Plan may be improved.*

THIS fcheme, if it has any thing of value in it, may undoubtedly be *improved*; and, perhaps, the indirect and collateral refults from it may be as confiderable as its direct and immediate effects.

I AM not, however, fo fond of my plan as to make an unqualified fuppofition that it is capable of producing fuch great advantages as I have defcribed. Yet I do not mean to conceal that I have a ftrong confidence in it; and I own, if I were to indulge

indulge my prefent thoughts, I fhould fay much more of the advantages I expeƈt from it.

Sect. XI.—*General Obfervations.*

But I fhall now only make a few GENERAL OB-SERVATIONS, which fhall conclude this Letter, and the trouble which, SIR, you have alloweu me to give you.

Firſt, IN A COMMERCIAL COUNTRY THERE SHOULD BE AS LITTLE DEAD OR UNPRODUCTIVE CAPITAL AS POSSIBLE : but the wealth of individuals colleƈted in the funds is *dead to trade and general uſe,* except only fo far as the dividends are fpent and circulated, and not invefted in the fame funds by way of farther accumulation.

And, *fecondly,* THERE OUGHT TO BE NO SUCH THING KNOWN AS WANT OF MONEY ;—and, in my opinion, no fuch want *could* be known in a perfeƈtly well-regulated commercial ſtate : I mean no want of that kind fhould be known or felt by thofe who poſſefs property of any kind, whether it confiſts of lands, merchandize, or credits well fecured. All fuch property fhould enable the owner to procure a REPRESENTATIVE SIGN capable of general circulation. I fay this, fubjeƈt to many obvious RESTRICTIONS.

Sect. XII.—*Originality of the Plan.*

It was, by thinking for a long time upon thefe two principles, and by turning over in my mind feveral plans for procuring money for fome perfons of property, who found it difficult to obtain Loans, that I was led to the prefent Discovery, if it is one, as I believe it to be. To me, at leaft it is *new,* and fo it has appeared to thofe friends to whom I have communicated it : but if any one fhall difpute the abfolute originality of the thought, I fhall not be much concerned about that, becaufe it is quite certain that in its operation it will be new, and, what is infinitely more material, the advantages of it will be confined, almoft exclufively, to our own Country, where alone fuch a great capital as I have propofed to put in circulation is to be found.

I have the honor to be,

SIR,

London,   &c. &c. &c.
Sept. 27, 1798.

A METHOD

OF

Increasing the Quantity

OF

CIRCULATING-MONEY:

Upon a new and folid Principle.

LETTER II.

ADVERTISEMENT.

The measure suggested in the First Letter on this subject having been approved of by a very great number of those who are best qualified to judge of it,—including persons of ALL ranks and parties, without distinction;—I consider it as a tribute of respect due to those who have given their sanction to the general idea of the plan, to submit to them the following detail of its proposed practical application, together with answers to some objections:—my design, in respect to the distribution of this Letter, being to limit it, for the present, to those persons whose opinions and suggestions upon it, as a sketch still admitting of IMPROVEMENT, I am desirous of obtaining.

24th JUNE 1799.

CONTENTS

OF THE

SECOND LETTER.

A 3   SECT.

A ME-

A

M E T H O D,

&c. &c. &c.

SECT. I.—*Proof of the Neceſſity of an Extenſion of the Circulating Medium; which had been before aſſumed.*

SIR,

In my former letter upon the ſubject of my propoſal of *a method of increaſing the quantity of circulating money*, I aſſumed the neceſſity of the meaſure to be ſelf-evident to thoſe who give attention to the whole circumſtances of the caſe: but, as I find there are *ſome* who deny the want of an increaſe of circulating money, I ſhould wiſh to remind thoſe perſons, that they have overlooked ſeveral important conſiderations. It is evident they pay no degree of attention to the impracticability of *borrowing money on* LANDED SECURITY, in conſequence as well

of

of the high rate of intereſt obtainable from Government ſecurities, and the expectation of future gain
by the riſe of ſtocks, as of the great profits which
trade affords; by the operation of which cauſes,
the WHOLE circulating capital of the nation is drawn
away from land to thoſe more profitable cbjects;
except what is taken up on ANNUITIES,—the moſt
pernicious mode of raiſing money, but at this time
the *only* expedient by which land-owners can borrow.

THE perſons who maintain that there is at preſent
no want of money alſo overlook the poſſibility (*or
rather the certainty*) that at ſome period, not very
diſtant, TRADE itſelf will again feel that diſtreſs
from the obſtructed circulation of money, which
occaſioned ſuch extremely ſerious alarm in 1793
and 1796, and the early part of 1797.

I SAY this without ſuppoſing a want of general
proſperity in the country: the diſtreſs I allude to
may even be cauſed by the increaſe of the commerce of the nation, which poſſibly may yet be
doubled; but certainly not without wanting a double
capital in money.

THE late ſudden and great increaſe of taxes will
alſo require an addition to be made to the circulating medium.—The GOLD withdrawn from circulation muſt alſo be ſupplied by PAPER.

THE

THE unufual facility with which money, or Bank-paper, which is *money* whilft it circulates *as fuch*, has been procureable for fome time paft by perfons of good credit, by way of difcount of commercial fecurities, is chiefly a temporary confequence of the preparation of money to be employed in the Government loan which was eagerly expected during the late winter and fpring. We all re-member the difappointment of the money-lenders in November laft, when Government borrowed only three millions out of fourteen that the loan was expected to confift of. Since that time, no doubt, there has been plenty of money for tempo-rary occafions, but not to lend on mortgages or on perfonal fecurity, apart from trade. Thefe very opulent perfons, who boaft of fuch an abun-dance of money, will not inveft any part of it in purchafing the land-tax, nor in loans to private perfons; except in difcounting bills or notes for the fhort period of fixty days, from which there refults a greater gain than five per cent. per annum.

PERMANENT LOANS, fuch as are adapted to the flow returns of agriculture, and cannot yield more than the legal rate of intereft,—thefe they utterly decline: and for an obvious reafon.— Land-owners have no means of giving more than five per cent. intereft,—except by the

deftructive

deſtructive means of granting *annuities* before taken notice of; but *perſons in trade* feel no difficulty in holding forth to *bankers* the temptation of more than the ſtatute-rate of intereſt upon loans of money, by means which *cuſtom* warrants, and which the *profits* of trade are more than equivalent to.

No perſon who has been much accuſtomed to tranſact loans on *mortgages* will deny the want of money, even its entire abſence, in *that* channel of circulation; nor can any perſon who is moderately converſant with what paſſes in Weſtminſter-Hall be uninformed of the diſtreſs which this want of circulation occaſions to thoſe who, having formerly lent money on land, now want to have it returned, as well as to the unfortunate debtors, who cannot find perſons to aſſiſt them in paying off their debts by taking transfers of the exiſting mortgages. It is well known to conveyancers that mortgage debts are *moſt commonly* diſcharged (even when money circulates freely) by transfers to other mortgagees, and not by actual payment on the part of the land-owners, who are *ſeldom* capable of redeeming their lands : more frequently payment is made by ſelling the incumbered eſtates.

Sect. II.—*Danger of the Landed Interest.*

WITHOUT fomething done to affift the LANDED INTEREST, the property in land will change hands almoft univerfally, or to a great extent, within a few years : lands will be brought to fale through the preffure of general diftrefs on the part of the land-owners, and the price, which was for fome time kept up by peculiar caufes, will then fall very low.

IT is beginning to fall already ; and I have been well informed that an uncommon proportion *in value* of the eftates put up to fale by auction within the laft year and more, have been bought in for want of purchafers at a fair price.

IT is high time that the land-owners fhould begin to look carefully to their own accommodation in refpect to the circulation of money; otherwife they muft be ruined. This is ftating the cafe without exaggeration ; for the merchants are getting vaft fortunes, whilft the land-owners are dwindling into comparative infignificance, and are in no fmall danger of becoming " hewers of " wood and drawers of water" to their rivals, the men of trade.

I SHOULD

I SHOULD not ſtate the matter in theſe ſtrong terms, if I had not a full conviction that the landed intereſt, a very great part of it, is in imminent danger from the circumſtances above ſet forth ; and if I did not know that ſtating the caſe in a cold manner, deſtitute of energy, would utterly fail to produce any effect upon that claſs of ſociety to which this part of the ſubject is peculiarly addreſſed.

FOR there are natural and permanent qualities in the character of the landed gentry of every country which cauſe them to give a languid attention to their intereſts *as a body*; the indolent and tranquil enjoyment of a revenue coming to them almoſt ſpontaneouſly, without much thought or any labour, having naturally the effect of indiſpoſing them to the conſideration of danger at a diſtance.

THEREFORE I cannot reaſonably expect to be much liſtened to by thoſe who are moſt concerned in what I am now ſaying, unleſs ſome of their own order, or others whoſe judgment they are accuſtomed to reſpect, ſhall ſupport me in warning them of their danger, and at the ſame time recommend the propoſed means of relief; or until a nearer approach of the miſchief, with ſome feeling of it, ſhall awaken their attention.

SECT.

SECT. III.—*Correction of a wrong Suppofition made by fome Perfons.*

IT has been fuppofed by fome perfons that, becaufe I have, in my former Letter, mentioned *fifty millions or more* as the fum which my fcheme *might* furnifh for the purpofes of circulation, it was my view to have fuch a large fum of money put into circulation whether the occa-fions of the country required it or not; and upon this miftaken fuppofition they have argued, that a proportionable increafe of the prices of com-modities would take place. But I have not propofed any thing like this, though I admit I might have excluded fuch a fuppofition in terms more guarded and lefs liable to be mifunderftood. I did not however fpeak quite incautioufly; for, after mentioning fifty millions or more, I added, " *if* " *fo much could be* EMPLOYED :" and in a former paffage, I had propofed the fcheme to be put in practice upon the ground and within the limits of *neceffity* and *utility*, which I thought a fufficient in-timation of the moderate ufe I wifhed to be made of the plan. But even if I had contemplated an immediate iffue of fuch a vaft quantity of paper money, it would not have raifed any fair objection to the principle of the meafure ; and indeed the

whole

whole objection is only applicable to the abuse of the plan, and takes for granted that it is to be acted upon without regard to ordinary discretion.

SECT. IV.—*Prices of Commodities not inconveniently raised by Paper-Money.*

THERE are others who have contended, that an inconvenient increase of the prices of all commodities would take place, if *any* addition were made to the quantity of circulating-money. To this I answer as follows:

THE increase of money would not, I think, have the effect of *raising prices* in respect to the NECESSARIES of life, because the *quantities* of them (supposing the money judiciously applied by bringing more land into cultivation) would be *increased* in a greater proportion than the money; yet I do not deny that such articles of luxury or curiosity as cannot be increased in quantity by cultivation or manufacture, would advance in price: but I suppose this will not be much insisted upon.

FURTHER, this objection might with equal reason be urged against any other measure which should tend gradually to increase the money of the country; and

and yet such an increase has been at all times, and probably will always continue to be, an object of eager pursuit, notwithstanding the supposed increase of prices consequent thereon.

In fact, a moderate increase of prices is not an evil; for such an increase tends to the extension of agriculture and manufactures, and to stimulate industry in every possible way, and therefore is a great benefit to a country by augmenting the quantity of its commodities; and this, by its reaction, prevents the rise of prices from being too rapidly accelerated.

Even high prices are only disadvantageous when they are occasioned by a permanent, or an extreme scarcity of commodities, or a very sudden scarcity, that is, when the demand continues for a long time, or in a very uncommon degree, or suddenly happens to exceed the supply; and, in general, a period of high prices is soon followed by abundance, and sometimes by extraordinary cheapness; the high price operating as an incitement to produce new and greater quantities of the commodity which yields an unusual profit.

Add to which, that the rise of prices is, in a great degree, an imaginary evil, so far as adding to the stock of money may be supposed to occasion the
increase

increafe of prices; for, in general, every man's fhare of money would be increafed too. The price of labour would rife as well as other things; and this joint increafe would caufe new exertions of diligence, by inciting or obliging many perfons to work who are now idle, or to work with greater diligence than before.

I EXCEPT, however, the cafe of perfons who live on fixed incomes, which they are incapable of enlarging. To them, every increafe of prices cannot but be a difadvantage. It is an unavoidable inconvenience, neceffarily attendant upon the ftationary pofition they hold. But it is not to be expected that the general progrefs of fociety is to be retarded, in order that thefe perfons may feel no manner of inconvenience from the circumftances which keep them in a ftate of inactivity, or hinder them from bettering their fortunes. The vigour of the nation cannot be kept down to the *par* of their imbecility; nor would this finally be any benefit to them, but very much the contrary: even if all neighbouring countries fhould, by univerfal agreement, confent to be ftationary too,—ceafing their progreffion in the arts and enjoyments of life. However, in the end, even perfons thus circumftanced would,—I mean *many* of them, —derive advantage from the operation of the plan,

by

by partaking, from collateral and accidental caufes, in the general profperity; and *all* of them would be eafed by the reduction of taxes, which would be one of the moft probable and moft extenfive confequences of the propofed meafure, as more fully noticed in a fubfequent part of this Letter.

Sect. V.—*The Advantages of the Plan, how to be difpofed of.*

It has been faid, I underftand, by fome perfons, that there is a *partiality* in giving to the ftockholders the great advantages I have fpoken of.

I have faid the emoluments to refult from the plan ought to be divided between the Stock-Proprietors, the Bank of England, and the Government, (that is, the nation at large,) in fuch proportions as may be agreed upon; of courfe, in juft and equitable proportions. Surely *fome* fhare of the advantages muft be given to the ftock-transferrers, and fufficient to induce them to engage their property in the execution of the fcheme. This is all that I have in view, or have fuggefted.

And this may be done in the following manner: —Let the privilege of iffuing the propofed notes

c   be

be given to the Subfcribers to FUTURE GOVERN-
MENT LOANS: and as the Subfcribers, with
this *bonus* given to them, would take the loans on
better terms, in proportion to the advantages they
obtained, *the whole Public* would by that means
largely participate in the profit to refult from the
fcheme.

SECT. VI.—*How the Plan may be applied to the Relief of the Landed Intereſt.*

My defign from the beginning was, and ftill is,
to accomplifh, if I am able, the procuring of
affiftance to thofe who want money upon the fecurity of land to enable them to pay their debts, or
to improve their eftates; and even this not for
their fakes only, but for the general good of the
country.

IF the fcheme I have propofed fhould take a
more extenfive range, and become applicable to
other purpofes befides the relief of the landed
intereft, it will be an accidental refult. I was
looking for one thing, and it may turn out that I
have found another of more importance; or rather
an application of what I had in view to a more
important fubject. I believe this is what commonly happens in fuch cafes.

BUT

BUT (in relation to the landed interest), I think the plan in question may be adapted to the accommodation of the LAND PROPRIETORS in the following manner:

LET the persons who are to obtain the notes upon the security of their transferred stock engage to lend the notes upon MORTGAGES of LAND, and to deposit the mortgages in the Bank of England within a limited time; their transferred stock being a security for the performance of this engagement. And let the Mortgages, when deposited, be declared by the act of the Legislature, which is to establish the whole measure, a further and collateral security for the amount of the circulating notes;— each mortgage for the amount of the notes lent thereon. Thus the note-creditor, however well satisfied he might be with the original security of the stock, would have another security of probably twice the amount of the notes,—a security far superior to that of an undefined, and, in some measure one may say, an imaginary quantity of gold deposited in a Bank. Every million of notes would be represented by four millions of stock and about two millions sterling in land!—I do not, however, mean to represent this ADDITIONAL security as NECESSARY to give strength to the original plan. I propose it as

c 2   subordinate

subordinate and convenient merely, not at all as being essential.

The mortgages when deposited would be capable of being transferred like other mortgages, but always subject to a general LIEN for the amount of the notes lent thereon; and might be discharged by bringing in to be cancelled an equal amount in notes of the same kind; these being cancelled, (that is, an equal amount, not the identical notes lent upon each mortgage,) the land might be reconveyed to the proper owner for the time being, discharged of the mortgage. And, at the same time, the transferred stock connected with the mortgage so released, might be re-transferred to the person to whom it should then belong.

By this means there would be a constant tendency of some portion of the notes to return into the Bank to be cancelled; which would prevent an excessive accumulation of the quantity; some periods might also be fixed for this purpose, and with this view; whereby the gradual and final extinction of the notes might be provided for, if a change of circumstances should require such extinction,

This operation of lending upon mortgages should be left, I think, to the discretion of the

INDI-

INDIVIDUALS by whom the loans are made, both in refpect to the titles to the mortgaged lands, and the quantity of fecurity, and, within fome limits to be prefcribed, the periods of repayment alfo; except that fome fuperintendence would be proper merely to afcertain that the loans were made bonâ fide upon the lands appearing in the feveral mortgages, and not employed for any other purpofe in the firft inftance.—Of which the depofit of the mortgages, with proper infpection, would furnifh good evidence.

THE rifk of the fecurity would upon this footing reft upon each individual lender; but that rifk, after the plan fhall have been acted upon for fome confiderable time, would be much lefs than it is now in fimilar loans; becaufe, as by the means propofed there would be eftablifhed a very extenfive *regifter of mortgages,* the difputes and frauds which too often attend fecurities of that nature would to a great degree be avoided.

THIS reftriction of the loans (fo long as it fhould be thought right to continue fuch reftriction) to landed fecurities would in itfelf limit the quantity of the propofed notes to the amount of the demand of money by land-owners defirous of borrowing. From them the money would be abforbed into the
general

general circulation, by payment of their debts, and by their making agricultural and other improvements.—By this means, alfo, tradefmen who are diftreffed for want of more early payment than they now receive, would be enabled to carry on their bufinefs and make their own payments with greater facility and more comfort than they can do at prefent.

SECT. VII.—*General Advantages.*

THUS, PUBLIC INDUSTRY would receive a new impulfe, employment would be given to many who are now in want of it, lands now unimproved and wafte would be brought into cultivation, houfes and other buildings would be repaired or erected, canals would be completed that are now left unfinifhed for want of money, bridges would be built, mines would be worked, NEW SOURCES of trade would be opened, and COMMERCE in a thoufand ways would be invigorated and put into a ftate of activity.

THIS may feem to fuppofe a more free ufe of the propofed money than could probably take place through loans on land only ; but in whatever way, or to whatever extent, the money fhould be employed, the mafs and quantity of ufeful and neceffary commodities,

commodities, and confequently the comforts of the people, would be increafed by this additional ftimulus given to the national exertion. This increafe would be proportionably greater than the increafe of money, fuppofing the latter to be added to with difcretion and by flow and gentle degrees, and not by an inundation of new reprefentative-figns; for it muft all along be borne in mind, that PUBLIC WISDOM is to direct the operation and to be employed in controlling the tides of this new money.

SECT. VIII.—*Effect of the Plan upon the Rate of Interest, and Reduction of the National Debt.*

ONE of the moft direct confequences to be expected from my plan, is the lowering of the RATE OF INTEREST. If it fhould be reduced generally below five per cent. that reduction would take away a part of the gain originally computed in the plan. But this would be counterbalanced by the good effects which a low rate of intereft always produces, and by other beneficial confequences which the plan may be made to accomplifh.

INDEED, this lowering of the rate of intereft would be, above all other means, I conceive, the
beft

beſt auxiliary to the fund eſtabliſhed by Parliament for relieving the nation from the preſſure of its GREAT DEBT.

A MOST happy event it would be, if the five per cent. ſtock could be reduced to four, and the other ſtocks in like proportion. A reduction to that extent would be the ſame thing in ſubſtance as a gratuitous extinction of a FIFTH PART of the NA-TIONAL DEBT; which conſiſts altogether, in re-ſpect to the right of demanding payment, in the ANNUITY payable by the nation to its creditors. Nor would it be difficult to effect a reduction to this amount by the help of the plan in queſtion; ſuppoſing the funds ſhall ever again come to the prices they were at in 1792; a ſuppoſition which this plan would alſo tend to realize. I admit that this reduction can only accompany the fall of the market-rate of intereſt.

THIS operation of diminiſhing the annual out-going might begin preciſely at the period when the SINKING FUND would loſe part of its beneficial efficacy, in reſpect to buying up the public debt, on account of the near approach of 3 per cent. ſtock to par; in which ſtock purchaſes could then no longer be made with advantage, till the whole of the 5 per cent. and 4 per cent. ſtocks ſhould be
bought

bought up. And though the latter ftocks would be above par, the public would derive no gain from that circumftance, though the ftock-holder might feem to fuftain a lofs by having his ftock paid off at par. But the near profpeût of fuch an event would keep thofe ftocks from attaining the prices they would otherwife reach.

As, at the period I am now fpeaking of, the annual produce of the SINKING FUND could not, for the foregoing reafons, be applied with great advantage in buying up the national debt, I fubmit it might then be better difpofed of, as a PREMIUM, in conjunûion with the PRIVILEGE of iffuing the notes in queftion, towards inducing monied men to lend large fums of money at a rate below the then current rate of intereft to be applied in paying off at par thofe debts which now carry a HIGH intereft. It will be foon found that I am not fpeaking without confideration when I talk of borrowing *below* the current rate of intereft, if that is not apparent already.

IN this way, though the *nominal* amount of the debt might continue to be the fame as before, ftill the nation would be relieved by the reduûion of the *annuity* in which the debt fubftantially confifts; and TAXES might then be repealed to a proportion-

able

able amount, or the SINKING FUND might be enlarged, fuppofing the whole taxes to be fuftained
fome time longer : or, the *faving* might be applied
in part to each of thefe objects.

To explain this propofed operation by an example :—Let us imagine an eftate to be incumbered with a debt of £. 100,000, at 5 per cent. intereft, or £. 5000 per annum. Then conceive the
owner to be poffeffed of £. 10,000 in ready money,
which if applied towards payment of the debt
would reduce it to £. 90,000, and the annual intereft to £. 4500. But the owner, having regard as
well to his own future convenience as to that of his
family after him, is defirous that his eftate fhould
be liable to a lefs annual outgoing; and therefore
propofes *to give the ten thoufand pounds* of which
he is poffeffed, *as a premium* to induce fome perfon
to pay off the debt on the eftate, and to accept a
transfer of the fecurity at a lower rate than 5 per
cent. And, in order further to abate the intereft,
he offers to give to the lender fome *extremely va-
luable privileges* of which he may be fuppofed to
have the command. Add to this an expectation
then formed, that the current rate of intereft will
fpeedily fall below 4 per cent. by the operation of
fome known caufes.

UNDER thefe circumftances, we may fuppofe that the new lender would advance his money at a lower rate than 5, or even than 4 per cent.—Grant it might be 3 per cent.—And if this fhould be the cafe, the annual incumbrance on the eftate will be reduced from £. 5000 to £. 3000.

I THINK the analogy is fo plain, that it is hardly neceffary to add that the £. 10,000 reprefents the produce of the *Sinking Fund* for a fhort period, fuppofe two or three years (more or lefs); and the *privileges* hinted at are correlative to the iffuing of notes to circulate as money on the credit of ftock.—The reft is quite obvious.

SUPPOSING this to be underftood and affented to, I may now go on to fay, that if, at the period above alluded to, the produce of the INCOME TAX fhould be applied in the fame manner towards the reduction of the rate of intereft, the *effect* produced in that way would be *greater*, and the *tax itfelf* might properly be made to ceafe *fooner*, than by its application towards extinguifhing the capital of the public debt.

AND in this refpect, as well as in the general tendency of the plan to produce an abatement of

taxes,

taxes, perfons of fixed incomes would have the fatisfaction of feeing their own advantage connected with the public welfare; a circumftance which I have before alluded to, and which I have great pleafure in thus explaining and confirming: for I am anxious that my propofal fhould produce nothing but GOOD; if that CAN be.

I ALLOW, that fo far as the produce of the *Sinking Fund* and that of the *Income Tax* are called in aid of this reduction of the annuity, the reduction would not be *gratuitous*; it is true:—but this does not hinder my firft fuggeftion on this point from being alfo true, namely, that the reduction in queftion might be brought about merely and folely by the help of this plan.—I believe it *might*, confidering the *command over the rate of intereft* which it would give to thofe who hold the reins of government: a moft important CONTROL *in the hands of thofe who are to manage on the part of the* DEBTOR !

YET it ftill may be proper to make the Sinking Fund and Income Tax co-operate to the fame end; by which means a greater and more fpeedy effect will be produced towards leffening the national debt, than could be managed by the unaffifted operation of this plan.

THERE

THERE certainly is not any thing that can fo effectually promote this reduction of the annual outgoing, as keeping the circulation of money conftantly full, and by that means lowering the rate of intereft; which hitherto there has not exifted the means of doing, but which by a right ufe of my plan may be accomplifhed: and this makes it be, what I humbly conceive it is,—*a great political engine*; in a word, A NEW POWER. I cannot refrain from faying *fo much*; for either it is THAT, or it is NOTHING.

SECT. IX.—*Bank of England.*—*How this Plan may be connected with it.*

IT appears from the evidence before the SECRET COMMITTEE on BANK AFFAIRS, that there were times within the ten years which preceded the Bank's ceafing to make payments in cafh, when the directors *deliberated* on reducing the rate of difcount: but they never did it; and though the reafons why they did not are left to be conjectured, it appears to me moft clear that one of the principal caufes which hindered the eftablifhment of that falutary regulation, was an uncertainty on the part of the Bank, whether they could conftantly keep the circulation full, or whether they might venture to

encourage

(30)

encourage the abundant circulation which a low rate of intereſt would tend to promote.

How ſoon, under the preſent circumſtances, the Bank may again think fit to leſſen the amount of their *diſcounts*, I do not pretend to conjecture; but ſome conſiderable effect in that way might probably be produced by a repeal of the preſent reſtriction on the iſſue of *caſh*.

I now come to ſhew how my plan may be connected with the eſtabliſhment of the BANK of ENGLAND.

I SUBMIT that THAT BANK, though it has peculiar intereſts of its own, may be moulded to purpoſes of public utility within the limits of a juſt and reaſonable regard to thoſe its intereſts. It OUGHT NOT to ſtand in the way of the general good of the community.

THEREFORE, with due regard to the Bank intereſts, I go on to ſay that there ought to be a PROPORTION between the Bank capital and effects, and the amount of the notes circulated on the credit thereof.

I PRESUME to ſuggeſt, that THAT PROPORTION ſhould be publicly *known* and *regulated by law*.

This

This *publicity* would at all times protect the Bank against a *run* upon it, which can only proceed from panic fears and a diftruft of its fecurity, occafioned by ignorance of its actual fituation.

THE amount of the circulating notes of the Bank, that is to fay, *circulating on the credit of the Bank capital*, ought never to exceed a *fixed* fum; let us fuppofe twelve millions.

ALL circulating bank paper *beyond* that amount ought to reft on other fecurity.

Now to apply thefe principles; let the Bank iffue its own notes inftead of the notes I have called ftock-notes. Let there be no diftinction.

BUT let the Bank be *permanently protected* by law againft paying CASH beyond the amount of its own proper or reftricted quantity of notes—*its own debt*—the twelve millions above mentioned.

Now fuppofe twenty millions to be in circulation, or any given fum exceeding twelve millions, the Bank might be liable (fuppofing the prefent reftriction taken off) to be called upon for *cafh* to the amount of twelve millions; — but the furplus fum they could not be required to pay in cafh;

cash; therefore they could not say their own establish-
ment was endangered by the additional quantity of
notes circulated on the credit of stock.

But if twenty millions were in circulation, the general call on the Bank for cash may be suppofed to
be proportionably greater than if only twelve millions
circulated; therefore the Bank muft keep a greater
proportion of gold in their treafury to carry on its
bufinefs; and for this, as well as for the management of the additional iffue of notes, the Bank
fhould receive a compenfation, including a reafon-
able profit.—I fhall for the prefent reft the matter
here fo far as concerns the Bank, conceiving that
all its effential interefts are thus fully taken care of.

SECT. X.—*The Security and Convenience to the*
Public under this Plan.

In refpect to the PUBLIC, I cannot difcover any
objection that they can make to the increafed circulation of bank notes upon the principles now
laid down. They have been content with an almoft
total reftriction of the iffue of gold in payment of
bank notes, and why fhould they not be equally
well content with having a moderate proportion of
thofe notes permanently exempted from being
paid

paid in cafh, there being other and moft abundant fecurity for their amount?—To fuppofe any inconvenience, one muft make a previous fuppofition that all the notes of the Bank of England, circulating upon the credit of their own capital, are required to be paid in cafh, with a fettled purpofe not to let it return there. But this fuppofes the natural death of the Bank; a perpetual ceffation of its ufe as a bank: a moft chimerical fuppofition! But even granting this infinitely improbable event to take place, ftill the furplus quantity of notes would be reprefented by a fourfold quantity of ftock and a double value in land, and thefe remaining notes would then be more convenient and neceffary than ever: for the Bank of England notes, its own proper and reftricted quantity, being fuppofed extinguifhed, the furplus notes would be effentially neceffary to the purpofes of COMMERCE, if any were fuppofed to remain.

THESE NOTES WOULD THEREFORE CONTINUE TO CIRCULATE; and by fuitable provifions to be made by the Legiflature at that time, might be liquidated in gold and filver as occafion might require. To fuppofe the contrary, is to fuppofe trade annihilated and all occafions for remittances from place to place within Great Britain to be put an end to for ever. So that it is only by imagining feveral events to take place, each

or

of them involving very high degrees of impro-
bability, that the circulation of the propofed notes
once begun can be expected ever to ceafe.

The fuppofition of the extinction of that quantity
of notes which is peculiarly to belong to the Bank of
England, I need hardly fay is made by way of argu-
ment, and not with any expectation of its ever
being realized. But the very putting of fuch a cafe,
even in this way, may appear alarming to
fome; therefore, I might propofe that the
whole profits to refult from the new quantity
of notes fhould be, annually or half yearly, fub-
jected in the firft place to indemnify the Bank of
England againft fuch lofs or detriment as this
fcheme may bring upon them; that indemnity
being made good out of the dividends of the
transferred ftock. I believe fuch a guarantee
(under circumftances fo very improbable) from
the new fyftem to the old one, would not de-
prive the former, the new fyftem, of any part
of its efficacy, or caufe the ftock-proprietors to
abate their expectations of gain from the operation
of the fcheme. The effect of fuch arrangement
would be, that the Bank of England would have
conftantly a profit upon twelve millions, or whatever might be the reftricted or the actual amount
of their circulation, not exceeding twelve millions;
and the ftock transferrers would have the profit upon

13   whatever

whatever might at any time be the additional quantity; fubject, in refpect to the latter, to a proper
deduction out of the dividends of the transferred
ftock for the charges of management and otherwife
in favour of the Bank.—I believe this will appear
eafily intelligible to thofe who will take the trouble
of thinking a little upon the point: but I am fen-
fible this part of the cafe requires rather more
attention than the reft.—It is, however, of the
leaft confequence, as it applies only to the moft
improbable of all the fuppofitions which the cafe
requires to be made: and if it creates a difficulty
in the mind of any reader, it may be paffed over,
without any difadvantage to the right comprehen-
fion of the fcheme: for it is only an anfwer to a
very refined and even imaginary objection.

Sect. XI.—*Conclufion.*

But, the original queftion recurs:—Is there a *want*
of circulating-money? And alfo the other queftion,
—Will the *Public* receive and circulate *thefe* notes
as cafh?—Concerning both of which queftions, if
I expreffed naturally and without referve all that I
think and feel, I fhould manifeft fuch a degree of
confidence of having made good what I have had in

view,

view, as would fcarcely feem confiftent with that deference with which I mean, Sir, to fubmit the whole matter to your fuperior difcernment; as I muft ultimately do to the JUDGMENT of the Public.

FOR the fake of brevity, and for other reafons, I have omitted fome things that might be faid in confirmation of my pofitions, and perhaps even fome explanations that may be thought neceffary by thofe who are fond of minute ftatements; but I think it beft to leave the matter here.—Permit me, therefore, to conclude with what I cannot but think very honourable to myfelf—I mean, a declaration of the fincere and refpectful attachment with which I am bound ever to be,

SIR,

Your devoted and faithful fervant,

&c. &c. &c.

LONDON,
18th June 1799.

POSTSCRIPT.

A SMALL number of Copies of this Second Letter having been diftributed, I have the fatisfaction to find it is allowed, by perfons in whofe judgment I have great reafon to confide, that the SCHEME is PRACTICABLE, and may prove USEFUL *in its prefent fhape.*—But I neither expect nor defire its adoption till the neceffity of it fhall be generally acknowledged.—Perhaps the univerfal admiffion of this neceffity is very near at hand ; for at this moment an uncommonly great *Scarcity of Money* (fuch as was predicted in page 8. of this Letter) is felt in TRADE, as well as by the LANDED INTEREST; and this Scarcity, if permitted to continue and increafe, (which it will do, unlefs checked by timely precautions,) will be productive of extremely diftreffing CONSEQUENCES.

THERE were inferted, in the diftributed Copies of this Letter, fome particular *objections* which had been made to the propofal, as ftated in the firft Letter, together with anfwers thereto. Thofe objections are now omitted, the latter part of the Letter which contained them having been re-printed
for

for that purpofe.—This was done in compliance with a wifh from the quarter from which the objections were communicated to me.

I HAVE not heard of any other objections which, in my opinion, (judging with as perfect an indifference as I am able to do in my own cafe,) apply fairly and correctly to the plan; fuppofing the Explanations and Modifications contained in this Second Letter to be duly confidered.

24th Sept. 1799.

Printed by A. Strahan, Printers-Street, London.